MW00989146

To

The memory of

JOHN M. TILLEY

Officer in Confederate Army

Killed in action

COVER PHOTOGRAPHS

Oak Alley Plantation in Vacherie, Louisiana

1-800-44ALLEY or www.oakalleyplantation.com

Facts The Historians Leave Out

By John S. Tilley, m.a. (Harvard)
Author of
Lincoln Takes Command
The Coming of the Glory
and
Alabama Equity Pleading and Practice

Nippert Publishing
1507 5 th Ave West
Springfield, Tenn. 37172
(615) 382-0444

FIRST PRINTING, DEC. 1951
SECOND PRINTING, JAN. 1952
THIRD PRINTING, FEB. 1952
FOURTH PRINTING, SEPT. 1952
FIFTH PRINTING, OCT. 1953
SIXTH PRINTING, OCT. 1954
SEVENTH PRINTING, JULY 1955
EIGHTH PRINTING, JULY 1956
NINTH PRINTING, JULY 1957
TENTH PRINTING, DEC. 1958
ELEVENTH PRINTING, FEB. 1960
TWELFTH PRINTING, FEB. 1961
THIRTEENTH PRINTING, APRIL 1963
FOURTEENTH PRINTING, JULY 1964
FIFTEENTH PRINTING, OCT. 1965
SIXTEENTH PRINTING, SEPT. 1967
SEVENTEENTH PRINTING, APRIL 1971
EIGHTEENTH PRINTING, MARCH 1983
NINTEENTH PRINTING, MARCH 1984
TWENTIETH PRINTING, MARCH 1988
TWENTY-FIRST PRINTING, MARCH 1990
TWENTY-SECOND PRINTING, AUGUST 1991
TWENTY-THIRD PRINTING, DECEMBER 1992
TWENTY-FOURTH PRINTING, NOVEMBER 1993
TWENTY-FIFTH PRINTING, JULY 1995
TWENTY-SIXTH PRINTING, MAY 1999

COPYRIGHT, 1951
JOHN S. TILLEY

COPYRIGHT, 1993
WILLIAM M. COATS

HOW OUR NATION WAS BORN

FIVE great movements ushered in the birth of the nation.

1. The First Continental Congress, which sent to the English King our declaration of rights. Its President was Peyton Randolph.

2. The agitation for armed resistance. Its leader was Patrick Henry.

3. The Declaration of Independence. Its author was Thomas Jefferson.

4. The War of The Revolution. Our Commander-in-Chief was George Washington.

5. The adoption of the Constitution. Its "father" was James Madison.

Does it signify anything that Randolph, Henry, Jefferson, Washington, and Madison all were Southern men?

Some other contributions. Jefferson promoted the Louisiana Purchase, nearly doubling the area of the United States. In a critical period, Andrew Jackson led our armies to victory at New Orleans. Polk guided our government during the War with Mexico and led to our securing about one million square miles of new Territory including Texas, New Mexico, and California. John Marshall was chiefly responsible for the early prestige of our Supreme Court.

Jefferson, Jackson, Polk, Marshall, all were Southerners.

Call the roll of our Presidents during the period between The War of the Revolution and the War Between the States. Four of the first five, seven of the first ten, ten of the first sixteen Presidents of the United States were sons of the South.

The brilliant Southern record came to a tragic end in 1861. Since that date, The South has been the nation's step-child.

WAS THE WAR OF THE SIXTIES FOUGHT OVER THE ISSUE OF SLAVERY?

DID THE North fight the war to free the slaves? That is a fair question. Maybe, you have come to believe that such a motive inspired the terrible struggle.

But, was that the cause?

Of all the leaders of that period, who do you think best qualified to know the true answer? Would not it have been Abraham Lincoln?

And, what do we learn from him?

He had served in Congress with Alexander H. Stephens of Georgia. On December 22, 1860, just two days after South Carolina left the Union, he wrote to Mr. Stephens:

"Do the people of the South really entertain fears that a R e p u b l i c a n administration would, directly or indirectly, interfere with their slaves, or with them about their slaves? If they do, I wish to assure you, as once a friend, and still, I hope, not an enemy, that there is no cause for such fears."

On the next fourth of March he became President. Had he changed his mind? Just after he took the oath of office, he said in his inaugural address:

"I declare that I have no intention, directly or indirectly, to interfere with slavery in the states where it exists."

Not only that. In 1862, when the war had been in progress for more than a year, Republican senators urged him to take action to free the slaves. He answered:

"Gentlemen, I can't do it . . . But I'll tell you what I can do; I can resign in favor of Mr. Hamlin. Perhaps Mr. Hamlin could do it."

There is the record. Was Mr. Lincoln, then, in favor of slavery? He was not. He believed it to be wrong and was opposed to allowing it to expand into **new states**; but, he thought he had no right to interfere with it in the states in which it **already existed.**

DID THE SOUTHERN ARMIES
FIGHT TO PRESERVE SLAVERY?

R OBERT E. LEE was the South's leading General. Not only had he freed the slaves under his control, but he had declared that slavery was "a moral and political evil." It was his view that "the best men in the South" opposed the system, and that they would welcome a sane movement to be rid of it. He was convinced that, in time, "the mild and melting influence of Christianity", rather than war, would solve the problem.

Stonewall Jackson agreed with Lee's view. He wished to see the shackles struck from every slave.

So, clearly, these great leaders of the Confederates were not fighting to retain a system which they hated.

What of the soldiers who marched behind Lee and Jackson? Bear in mind that only one in fifteen of Southern whites ever owned a slave. All in all, there were fewer than 350,000 Southern slave-owners.

But there were some 600,000 soldiers in the Confederate Armies. So, if all the slave-owners were in uniform— and, certainly, they were not — this still leaves several hundred thousand soldiers with no personal interest in slavery.

What were these non-slaveholders fighting for?

Investigation will reveal that not only Colonel Robert E. Lee, whose troops captured John Brown at Harper's Ferry, and Governor Henry A. Wise, in whose State of Virginia Brown was executed, but a majority of Virginians were sincerely opposed to slavery.

Southern opposition to slavery was not something new. Daniel Webster once declared that the leading spirits of the South regarded it as "an evil, a blight, a scourge, and a curse." He might have called the roll, a roll including such names as Washington, Jefferson, M a d i s o n, Monroe, Wythe, Richard Henry Lee, Patrick Henry, John Randolph, and George Mason.

WHO IMPORTED THE SLAVES
FROM AFRICA?

O F COURSE, slavery was an ugly blot on American history. And, you know that many Southerners owned slaves; so, our section deserves its share of the blame.

But, how did the slaves get here?

That's a question which, even though your histories are strangely silent, you would like to have answered.

British and Dutch vessels engaged in the slave trade, and by slave trade is meant bringing them over from Africa. But, there were also American ships in the ugly business; and, though the historians have carefully steered clear of the fact, practically every one of them was owned and operated by Northerners.

The Puritans of Massachusetts not only captured their Pequot Indian neighbors and sold them into slavery in the West Indies; they also carried on a large trade in negroes imported from over seas. Just to give you an idea, between 1755 and 1766, the importers landed on Massachusetts shores no fewer than 23,000 African captives.

In 1787, Rhode Island held first place in the traffic. Later, New York City forged to the front in the trade. Philadelphia soon found the slave-business attractive. The traders could buy a slave in Africa for a few gallons of rum and sell him in this country at a fantastic profit. So, it is no mystery how they made fabulous fortunes.

It was made unlawful to import slaves after the year 1808. Did this put a stop to the traffic?

If it did, why did Congress in 1820 brand the slave-trade as "piracy"? The answer is that Northern smugglers were bringing in each year some 40,000 Africans.

And why, in 1860, did President Buchanan boast that "since the date of my last annual message, not a single slave has been imported into the United States in violation of the law"?

And why, in 1861, long after the outbreak of

war and fifty-three years after the trade had been outlawed, did President Lincoln write to Congress that "five vessels, being fitted out for the slave trade, have been seized and condemned"?

And, how did it happen that in December 1858 a New York City slave-ship secretly landed 420 slaves on the coast of Georgia?

The answer to the questions is simple.

For easy money, Northern importers of slaves were openly defying the law.

And, what did the Northern traders do with their slaves?

They sold them to Southern planters. Thus it came about that, in the year 1860, there were in the South some 3,500,000 slaves for whom the Southern people had paid the Northern traders millions of dollars.

Coming back to Mr. Lincoln, it may interest you to learn that, over and over again, he freely admitted that, for the existence of slavery in this country, the North was as responsible as the South.

WERE SOUTHERN MASTERS BRUTAL
TO THEIR SLAVES?

B EYOND QUESTION, some masters cruelly whipped and abused their slaves. Every right-thinking Southerner is ashamed of that record.

Has it occurred to you that, even today, some husbands and fathers brutally beat their wives and children? That, however, doesn't prove that all husbands and fathers are brutes, does it?

And, at times, unruly children have to be punished. It was so with the slaves. Most of them were childlike, good natured, well-behaved. But, not all! There were those who were treacherous and dangerous and who could be controlled only by the use of force.

Consider that the only reason the planter bought slaves was that he needed them to work. If he paid $1,000.00 for a worker, would he be so shortsighted as to starve or mistreat him?

Fortunately, some foreigners visited t h e South in those days for study of the situation. B u c k i n g h a m, a distinguished Englishman, wrote that the slaves observed by him were as well off as were English servants in the middle rank of life. He found them "well-fed, well-dressed, and easy to be governed."

In 1856, Frederick L. Olmsted, a Northern student, published his Journey in the Seaboard Slave States. Noting that the situation might be different elsewhere, he wrote of slave conditions in sections visited by him. He learned that the slaves were probably fed better than any comparable class of other countries. The labor required of house-servants he described as light, that of field-hands not appreciably heavier than that of the laborer in the North. It interested him that slave marriages were frequently made occasions, attended by their owners; those of favorite slaves, performed in the master's house by the master's minister.

Now, while we are talking of cruelty, what of the Northern importers' treatment of the slaves? One of these days you should read a book which describes their trip over from Africa. Often, it recites, they were packed into tiny vessels from 60 to 70 feet in length; they were placed between decks where the intervening space was from 3 feet, 6 inches, to 3 feet, 10 inches; thus they had to sit or lie down, except that at times trusties were allowed above deck for exercise.

Get that picture! Think of the weeks-long voyage, the crowding, the heat between decks, the rough seas, the seasickness, the absence of bath or comfort rooms.

When Mr. Lincoln came to Washington in 1847, he found there slave-markets which he described as "a sort of negro livery stable." And, when he asked questions, he learned that the slaves were held there only until they could be sent to Southern markets.

One thing more. Have you ever wondered how it came about that nearly every member of the former slave-group became a Christian? Many of them were uncivilized in their African homes. But, after living for some years in close contact with their Southern owners, they embraced the Christian faith. Would they have adopted the religion of masters who were brutal to them?

THE EMANCIPATION PROCLAMATION

I F YOU haven't studied the Proclamation, you are headed for a shock when you read it carefully.

It says in so many words that it is "a fit and necessary **war measure for suppressing said rebellion.**" That means that Lincoln thought it would make it easier to subjugate the South.

It undertook to free the slaves only in the States and "parts of States" which were then in possession of the Confederate Government. It names ten Southern States but goes on to explain that it does not apply to West Virginia, or to thirteen named parishes of Louisiana, or to seven named counties of Virginia. As to these, it recites, "which excepted parts are for the present **left precisely as if this proclamation were not issued.**" The Northern armies had regained possession of the "excepted parts"; so their slaves were not **affected.**

If the Proclamation was a heaven-born movement, why were the slaves in the "excepted parts" left out? And, why did Lincoln delay issuing it until January 1, 1863, when the war had been in progress for nearly two years? And, why does it fail even to mention the states of Maryland, Kentucky, and Missouri? Why did it leave in slavery the slaves in those States?

Lincoln's performance amused Palmerston, Premier of England. Palmerston arose tauntingly to remark that Lincoln undertook to abolish slavery where he was without power to do so, while protecting it where he had power to destroy it.

One explanation was that the Proclamation would likely result in the crippling of the Confederate war effort. Slaves were used at the front in such tasks as digging of trenches. A revolt of slaves would bring collapse of Southern resistance. Hence, the "necessary w a r measure."

There was other inspiration. England and France were on the verge of recognizing the independence of the Confederate Government.

In 1862 the British Foreign Minister had written the Prime Minister: "The time has come for offering mediation to the United States Government with a view to recognition of the independence of the Confederates. In case of failure, we ought ourselves to recognize the Southern States as an independent State."

Catching the point, knowing the English aversion to slavery, Lincoln resorted to his grand gesture. Despite Palmerston's acrid comment, the agitation for recognition died.

To the South the war was one for independence. Woodrow Wilson appraised the Proclamation as an effort to shift the struggle into a crusade against a South championing the institution of slavery.

There were others who were not deceived. Edward Channing, the New England historian, was honest enough to write of the Proclamation: "Of course, it did not abolish slavery as an institution anywhere."

Had the Proclamation abolished slavery altogether, Lincoln's own family might have been

affected. For, his father-in-law was a slaveholder, and Mrs. Lincoln's share of her father's
estate was partly derived from the proceeds of
the sale of slaves.

"THE GREAT EMANCIPATOR'S"
ESTIMATE OF THE NEGRO

THE EMANCIPATION PROCLAMATION bears date January 1, 1863. It so happened that on August 14, 1862, less than five months before, there was an interesting conference at the White House. By invitation of Mr. Lincoln, a group of free negroes was there to hear his words of wisdom. Among other matters he discussed his purpose to colonize "people of African descent." Those present must have sat wide-eyed as they listened to his estimate of their race. The following was what they heard:

"Why should people of your race be colonized, and where? Why should they leave this country? This is, perhaps, the first question for proper consideration.

"You and we are different races. We have between us a broader difference than exists between almost any other two r a c e s. Whether it is right or wrong, I need not discuss; but this physical difference is a great disadvantage to us both, as I think. Your race suffers very greatly, many of them, by living among us, while ours suffers from your presence. In a word, we suffer on each side.

"If this is admitted, it affords a reason, at least, why we should be separated.

"You here are freemen, I suppose. Perhaps you have long been free, or all your lives. Your race is suffering, in my judgment, the greatest wrong inflicted on any people.

"But, even when you cease to be slaves, you are yet far removed from being placed on an equality with the white race. The aspiration of men is to enjoy equality with the best when free, but on this broad continent not a single man of your race is made the equal of a single man of ours."

The above is quoted solely to acquaint you with what **Mr. Lincoln** saw fit to say on that occasion.

WHY THE PLANTERS FOUGHT
TO KEEP THEIR SLAVES

IN THE EARLY period of the nation, there was little or no opposition to slavery. The North as well as the South adopted the Constitution with full knowledge that it recognized and protected the institution.

Later, the North began to get rid of its slaves, not by freeing them but by selling them to Southern planters. In time, there were several millions of slaves working on multiplied thousands of Southern farms. Agriculture became the principal business. When agriculture was successful, the Southerners as a whole prospered.

The day arrived when the South waked up to the fact that, deprived of the labor of the slaves, its entire business-structure would collapse, with ruin stalking the land. So, do you wonder that the planters held on grimly to their slave system?

Try an illustration. Suppose that y o u r father had patiently built up a successful business; that he had a splendid plant and a faithful group of employees. Then, suppose that some organization fathered a plan which would rob him of every employee. Do you think that he would submit without a struggle?

That is precisely what the Northern fanatics succeeded in doing with the South's agricultural labor. They freed, not all the labor on one plantation, but **all the labor on all the plantations.** They did this without paying the planters one cent.

To give you an idea of what this meant, in 1860 there were in the South some three and one-half million slaves; the value of the average able-bodied slave was about one thousand dollars. This was the investment completely wiped out by crusaders from the very section which had then, and still has, the purchase-money paid by the planters for their slaves.

WHAT ARE STATES' RIGHTS?

IN 1781, THE ORIGINAL thirteen States entered into a "Confederation", and drew up "Articles", one of which said:

"Each State retains its sovereignty, freedom and independence, and every power, jurisdiction, and right which is not by this Confederation expressly delegated to the United States."

That meant simply that the independent States were willing to join together as the "United States", and to give to this "Union" certain powers; but they carefully kept for themselves all other powers. This involves what are called States' Rights.

When the Revolutionary War ended, England and the "United States" signed a peace-treaty, which opened with these words:

"His Britannic Majesty acknowledges the said United States, viz., New Hampshire, Massachusetts Bay, Rhode Island and Providence Plantations, Connecticut, New York, New Jersey, Pennsylvania, Delaware, Virginia, North Carolina, South Carolina, and Georgia, to be free, sovereign, and independent States."

So, England made peace, not with the "Confederation", but with thirteen "independent" States.

To the Convention which considered a new "Constitution", Georgia's delegates c a r r i e d commissions which opened: "The State of Georgia, by the grace of God, Free, Sovereign, and Independent."

Those of the New York delegates closed: "This 9th day of May, in the 11th year of the Independence of the said State." Their commissions were issued in 1787, eleven years after the signing of the Declaration of Independence.

There is more than that. New York voted to accept the Constitution giving certain powers to Congress, but it added: "That the powers of government may be reassumed by the people, whensoever it shall become necessary to their happiness." That meant that, should it think such action necessary, New York reserved the right to leave the Union and to govern itself.

Also, Virginia, in its acceptance said: "The powers granted under the Constitution, being derived from the people of the United States, may be resumed by them, whensoever the same shall be perverted to their injury or oppression." Feeling injured and oppressed, Virginia and the other seceding States "resumed" those powers in 1861.

Article X of the Constitution itself says: "The powers not delegated to the United States by the Constitution, nor prohibited by it to the States, are reserved to the States respectively, or to the people."

The powers given the Congress were those necessary to protect the people of all the States, such as raising an army, coining money, regulating commerce. They did not give the United States the right to interfere in local problems, those in which only the citizens of a State were concerned.

Maybe, an example will help. Your home is in a town with a government to which your family looks for protection. You wouldn't, however, like for the town-government to dictate matters inside your home. Just so, the States felt that their own "local problems" could be managed without meddling from the outside.

It was only when the Washington Government began reaching out for too much power that the issue of States' Rights became important. States' Rights advocates are loyal to the United States, but they wish to be left alone to manage State affairs. They fear that in time the Washington Government may become all-powerful.

NORTHERN VIOLATION
OF STATES' RIGHTS

REMEMBER THAT THE Southern owners neither stole nor captured their slaves. They bought them largely from Northern slave-importers. There were thousands of Southerners who would have liked to see the slaves freed. But they realized that, without their labor, the South would be terribly crippled. With Robert E. Lee, they hoped that some fair solution could be found.

They did not, however, think it right that the North, which had grown rich by the traffic, should undertake to free them all at once and by force and without repaying one cent of the purchase-money.

Mr. Lincoln knew perfectly well that the Constitution recognized and protected slavery. But there were fanatics in the North who were unwilling to wait until the problem could be solved in a peaceable and lawful manner. What cared they for the Constitution? In 1854, one of their leaders, Garrison by name, celebrated the fourth of July, "Independence Day", by publicly burning a copy of the Constitution of the United States! He denounced it as "an agreement with hell."

The fire-eaters did more than preach hatred of slavery and hatred of the Southerners. They set out deliberately to incite the millions of slaves to rise against their masters. They flooded the Southern mails with dangerous appeals until President Andrew Jackson denounced them for trying "to produce all the horrors of a servile war." You can realize what this meant by recalling that one-third of the South's population were slaves.

The fanatics succeeded, succeeded all too well. For example, in Southampton County, Virginia, Nat Turner with sixty other slaves ran wild for two days and nights; they murdered Turner's owner, and the owner's family, and half a hundred other helpless victims.

Again, in 1859, John Brown, leading a band of armed conspirators, stormed the armory at Harper's Ferry, Virginia. They carried specially-made weapons **with which to arm the slaves.** It required a force of the United States Army to subdue and capture them.

Do you wonder that the prospect of slave-uprisings carried terror to every Southern fireside? This, and other acts of an unfriendly section, led the Southerners to form their own government, one which could and would afford protection for their families and homes.

WAS SECESSION TREASON?

YOU HAVE read that some Northerners demanded that Robert E. Lee be executed for treason. And, maybe you know that the captors of Jefferson Davis subjected the aged man to torture which would have done credit to a horde of savages.

Were Lee and Davis and their followers criminals because of their exercise of the right to secede?

Let us go again to Abraham Lincoln. He said in 1847 on the floor of Congress:
'Any people, anywhere, being inclined and having the power, have the right to rise up and shake off the existing government, and form a new one that suits them better. This is a most valuable, a most sacred right, a right which we hope and believe is to liberate the world."

Don't miss the point that 1847 was just thirteen years before the South began to secede.

If what Lincoln taught was good doctrine in 1847, why not in 1860? And, did not "any people, anywhere" take in the people of the South?

Little wonder that an English historian, Goldwyn Smith, commented that Southern secession could not have asked a clearer support than this statement by Lincoln.

Going further back: referring to the right to safety and happiness, the Declaration of Independence said:

"Whenever any form of government becomes destructive to these ends, it is the right of the people to abolish it, and to institute a new government."

And, a glance at some New England history may prove of interest.

In 1803, New England leaders grew white with rage over the idea of admitting Louisiana into the Union. Senator Plumer of New Hampshire said:

"The Eastern States must and will dissolve the Union and form a separate government of their own; and the sooner they do this, the better."

Senator Pickering of Massachusetts wrote: "I rather anticipate a new Confederacy exempt from the corrupt influence of the aristocratic Democrats of the South . . . There will be a separation . . . The British provinces (of Canada), even with the consent of Great Britain, will become members of the Northern Confederacy."

There you have it! A NORTHERN CONFEDERACY.

You haven't read much about **that** in your histories, have you? Their plan did not succeed but they tried to carry it out.

Then, in 1814, New England held its famous "Hartford Convention" which plainly considered secession from the Union.

Not only in 1814. Again in 1845, John Quincy Adams and fellow New Englanders so opposed the admission of Texas that they openly urged withdrawal from the Union.

1845 was just fifteen years before Southern secession.

Keep in mind that Virginia carefully reserved the right to leave the Union; all Southern States believed in such a right.

About the time of the graduation of Robert E. Lee and Jefferson Davis, West Point was using a text-book which left no doubt of the right of a State to withdraw.

So! When at last the South acted, it followed an example suggested by New England, first in 1803, again in 1814, and still again in 1845.

WAS GEORGE WASHINGTON
A TRAITOR?

CHARLES FRANCIS ADAMS was a member of the Adams family of Massachusetts. He wrote that, when the Constitution was adopted, it was fully understood that each State had the right to leave the Union.

Northern abuse of Robert E. Lee caused Adams to flame with indignation. "If Lee was a traitor," he said, "so also was George Washington."

What, indeed, was the American Revolution but a secession of the thirteen States from Great Britain?

Lay side by side the movements of 1776 and 1860. On the one hand the heavy burden of the Stamp Act tax, on the other the harsh unfairness of a sectional tariff. In 1776 the arrogance of the English, in 1860 the bitter abuse by the abolitionists. In Washington's day English assumption that talk of American independence was treason, in Lee's time the attitude of a hostile North that mention of separation from the Union was sedition. In the Revolutionary era the threat of the British to use their army and navy to prevent the colonies from breaking away from the Empire, in the Southern secession period the intention of the North to resort to force to hold the South in the Union.

Which, then, was glorious revolution and which infamous rebellion? What if the British had come to the aid of the South, as for a time they considered doing, and the South had emerged as an independent nation of States of which one alone was larger in area than England, France, Italy, or Germany?

In what respect of principle would the historian have found a difference between the War of Independence of 1776 and the War of Independence of 1861?

THE SOUTH FIRED THE FIRST SHOT

I<small>T</small> DID.

WHY?

After South Carolina exercised its right to secede, Fort Sumter at Charleston was manned by a Union garrison. The State demanded possession of the fort and offered to pay for it. Although the Secretary of State of the United States solemnly promised that the garrison would be removed, his Government failed to give the necessary order.

Resisting the temptation to take the fort by force, the Carolinians had nevertheless given fair warning that no reinforcement would be tolerated.

Under the pretext that he was sending "provisions" to the garrison, which at that very moment was being supplied by South Carolina with fresh meat, groceries, a n d vegetables, Lincoln assembled a fleet of war vessels carry-

ing supplies, guns and ammunition, and ordered it to Charleston.

Warned of the coming of the fleet, before
reinforcements could be thrown in, the Carolinians bombarded and captured Sumter. Better
than anyone else, Lincoln knew it to be a
practical certainty that this would be the result. There was no doubt that the cry, "The
South has fired on the Flag", would fire the
heart of the North.

A leading English editor wrote of Lincoln:
"He has thought that a political object was to
be obtained by putting the Southerners in the
wrong, if they could be maneuvred into firing
the first shot."

THE "STARVING GARRISON"

IDA TARBELL in her biography of Lincoln mentions a letter which she says Lincoln received from Major Anderson on March 4, 1861, the day of his inauguration. Asserting that it gave notice that the Sumter garrison's food would be exhausted **within a week,** she commented that the command must be **rescued from starvation.**

John T. Morse, in his **Abraham Lincoln,** refers to the same Anderson letter, saying that it disclosed the food supply at Sumter as being **a certain quantity of biscuit and pork,** probably enough to sustain the garrison for **about four weeks.**

Lincoln's Secretary of the Navy also mentions in his **Diary** the Anderson letter, stating that from it the President learned that the Sumter food stores were critically low, and that Anderson **could get no provisions in Charleston.**

The OFFICIAL RECORD, published by the

United States Government, discloses that, beginning January 20, 1861, the Governor of South Carolina arranged to supply the Sumter command with fresh meat, vegetables, and groceries.

The Record shows further that, in a report of March 20th., Anderson stated that he had written Governor Pickens on **March thirteenth** of his "failure to receive boxes of solidified milk" which had reached Charleston. The Governor promised an investigation.

On March 17th., Anderson wrote the Governor's representative:

"I hasten to ask you to refer to my letter to his Excellency, and you will see that I did not solicit **any modification** of his original permission about receiving supplies of fresh meat and vegetables. **I am satisfied with the existing arrangement** and only called attention to a reported interference of it."

WHO "BEGAN" THE WAR?

IN LINCOLN'S fourth annual message to the Congress, dated December 6, 1864, he wrote:

> "In stating a simple condition of peace, I mean simply to say that the war will cease on the part of the Government whenever it shall have ceased on the part of those who began it."

Let's see about that.

On April 4, 1861, when his reinforcement squadron was ready to sail, Lincoln drafted a "confidential letter" for Simon Cameron to send to Anderson. It notified the Commander that "the expedition will go forward." This referred to the reinforcing fleet of war vessels.

On April 7th., Anderson answered the letter, saying in part:

> "I ought to have been informed that the expedition was to come. Colonel Lamon's remark convinced me that the idea, merely hinted at to me by Captain Fox, would not

be carried out. We shall strive to do our duty, though I frankly say that my heart is not in the war which I see is thus to be commenced."

There is the testimony of the Union Commander of Fort Sumter. Surely, he was the one man best informed as to the exact situation.

Is there occasion for wonder that so many writers of the war story have seen fit to leave Anderson's verdict severely alone?

THOSE "FIRE-EATING" SOUTHERNERS

KNOWLEDGE that Lincoln's reinforcing squadron was on the way compelled the Southerners to act. On April 12th., Beauregard demanded evacuation of the fort. Anderson declined to comply. As the aides were leaving he remarked:

"I will await the first shot and, if you do not batter us to pieces, we will be starved out in a few days."

Anderson's statement meant that, cooped up in a fort, surrounded by Confederate batteries, he was caught in a trap; that the lives of every man of the command might be the price of resistance.

This was something else. The Southerners had sprung from stock which held in contempt a man who would shoot a bird on the ground. Beauregard repeated to Confederate Secretary of War Walker what Anderson had said. Walker promptly **revoked the order to attack, saying:**

"Do not desire needlessly to bombard Fort Sumter. If Major Anderson will state the time at which he will evacuate . . . you are authorized thus to avoid the effusion of blood."

Beauregard informed Anderson of Walker's offer. Anderson answered:
"I will evacuate Fort Sumter by noon of the 15th instant . . . should I not receive prior to that time controlling instructions from my Government, or additional supplies."

Anderson's concluding words closed the door. It had so happened that Lincoln's April fourth letter had informed Anderson:
"On the information of Captain Fox, he (the President) had supposed you could hold out till the 15th instant . . . and had prepared an expedition to relieve you before that period."

"THAT IS MAGNIFICENT, BUT THAT IS NOT WAR"

S O EXCLAIMED an observer, a French General, as he watched the charge of the Light Brigade. The Sumter bombardment supplied an occurrence of similar character.

When, in other days, Major Anderson taught at West Point, Cadet Beauregard showed such character and ability that Anderson retained him as Assistant Instructor. Later relations between the two became cordial, even intimate. Now, under different flags, they confronted each other as foes.

During the bombardment of Sumter, the wooden barracks caught fire. Dense clouds of black smoke indicated a serious conflagration. As he watched, Beauregard knew that if the flames reached the powder magazines, the resulting explosion would strew the surrounding sea with wreckage of Fort and fragments of bodies.

Let Beauregard's report tell the story:

"About 7½ o'clock it was discovered that

our shells had set fire to the barracks within the Fort . . . Apprehending some terrible calamity to the garrison, I immediately dispatched an offer of assistance to Major Anderson."

Bearing in mind that this merely interrupted the fighting, hear the report of Beauregard's aides:

"We found the barracks totally destroyed. . . . We stated to Major Anderson that we had been sent with a fire engine to offer assistance to extinguish the fire. The Major replied that his fire was almost burned out. We again asked if he did not think it best to use the engine which accompanied us on the steamer. He replied no — that he thought everything had been consumed that would burn . . . He asked us to thank General Beauregard for his kindness; and on leaving, the Major accompanied us himself as far as our small boat."

Some six hours later, the battle ended with the surrender of the garrison.

A SPECTACLE FOR THE GODS

IF, ON APRIL 15, 1861, the gods on Olympus chanced to be looking down on Charleston Harbor, they witnessed a scene which must have thrilled even them.

The bombardment of Sumter had continued for thirty hours. Through the hell of shot and fire and threatening disaster, the heroic Union garrison had stood doggedly by its guns.

On the thirteenth the Union resistance collapsed. Beauregard chose not to hold the garrison as captives; on the contrary, he extended them every courtesy. Major Anderson was given the privilege, not only of saluting his flag, but of marching his command out "with banners flying and with drums beating 'Yankee Doodle.'"

Nor was that all. The Confederate General provided a steamer, the **Isabel,** to transport Anderson and his men to the Union fleet anchored outside the harbor — the very fleet which had been sent to reinforce the Fort.

A sorrowful journey it was for the Union group. Presently, however, it developed that the occasion of their departure was not to be uneventful. From the shore-batteries streamed the artillerymen who, but a few hours before, had manned the guns which had made wreckage of Sumter.

From Beauregard's report, hear the conclusion of the story:

"When, on the 15th instant, he left the harbor on the steamer **Isabel,** the soldiers of the batteries on Cummings Point lined the beach, silent, and with heads uncovered, while Anderson and his men passed before them."

Pay tribute to the Yankees? To be sure they would — **and did!**

THE "RESULT" WHICH LINCOLN FORESAW

W OULD YOU LIKE conclusive proof that Lincoln's plan was to badger the Southerners into "firing the first shot"?

It was his Secretary of the Navy, Gideon Welles, who wrote: "It was very important that the Rebels strike the first blow in the conflict."

Lincoln assembled the squadron of warships and tugs, as recommended by Captain G. V. Fox. He placed Fox in command and sent the fleet to Charleston.

The reinforcement project had been outlined by Fox: "I simply propose three tugs convoyed by light-draft men of war . . . The first tug to lead in empty, **to open their fire.**"

Before Fox could carry out the plan, the Southerners bombarded and captured the fort.

Did the failure of the expedition distress

Lincoln? Not at all. On May 1, 1861, he wrote Fox:

> "I sincerely regret that the failure of the attempt to provision Fort Sumter should be the source of annoyance to you . . .
> "You and I both anticipated that the cause of the country would be advanced by making the attempt to provision Fort Sumter, **even if it should fail;** and it is no small consolation now to feel that **our anticipation** is **justified by the result.**"

WAS THERE SUFFERING
IN SOUTHERN PRISONS?

MUCH HAS BEEN WRITTEN about suffering in Southern prisons.

Strangely, the writers ignore the main reason for it.

Critics have complained bitterly of the poor quality of food provided. The fact is that the rations supplied the prisoners were the same as those issued to the Confederate soldiers in the field.

The time came when, shut off from the world by blockade, the South experienced the greatest difficulty in obtaining medicine which had been made contraband by order of the Federal government. By 1864 conditions became so desperate that the South actually offered to purchase from the North such needed supplies, agreeing to pay in gold, cotton, or tobacco. The offer made plain that Union surgeons might bring the medicines down and use them solely to minister to Union prisoners. **To this offer, there was no reply.**

The Union soldiers held in Southern prisons out-numbered by 50,000 the Confederates imprisoned in the North. This was revealed when, shortly after the war, Lincoln's Secretary of War issued a report showing that 26,246 Confederates died in Northern prisons as against 22,576 Union soldiers dying in Southern prisons.

A dependable authority says:
"It is indisputably established that the Confederate authorities constantly pressed exchanges on equal terms, that they proposed many measures of relief which were denied, that at length the most pitiable and unusual of all spectacles occurred when a deputation of Union soldiers appeared in Washington, sent by Mr. Davis, to plead for release by fair exchange, and to plead in vain.

In 1864, General Grant explained to General Butler:
"It is hard on our men held in Southern prisons not to exchange them, but it is humanity to those left in the ranks to fight

our battles. Every man released on parole becomes an active soldier against us at once. If we commence a system of exchange which liberates all prisoners taken, we will have to fight on until the whole South is exterminated. If we hold those caught, they amount to no more than dead men."

All of which adds up to this. The North, with overwhelming numbers, could easily replace captured men; the South had called up every available man and each soldier lost rendered it just that much weaker. So, those in authority in the North simply chose to abandon their captured comrades to their fate.

There is another story, one not so frequently told, the story of the Southern soldiers, in threadbare uniforms, who froze to death in Northern prisons.

"WITH MALICE TOWARD NONE—
WITH CHARITY FOR ALL."

(Lincoln inaugural, March 4, 1865)

AT FORT PICKENS, Florida, in 1861, Southern and Northern forces relied upon a formal agreement which sought to delay the opening of conflict. The **Southern Commander** had signed for the South, the **Secretaries of War and Navy** for the North. The Lincoln administration carried out a violation of this agreement.

Later, the administration provoked the South into firing on Fort Sumter. The theory was that only "provisions" were being sent to a hungry garrison. Along with provisions went reinforcements consisting of warships, troops, guns, and ammunition. It was a foregone conclusion that this would bring an attack on the Fort. Thus was begun a war which slaughtered hundreds of thousands of young men.

More than that. Lincoln was Commander-in-Chief of Northern forces when Sherman won his never-to-be-forgotten victory over the helpless women and children of Georgia. Of the campaign, Sherman himself wrote that his troops had done at least one hundred million dollars worth of damage, four-fifths of which, far from being of military advantage, was "simple waste and destruction."

Instead of censuring Sherman for disregard of the rules of civilized warfare in his march through Georgia, and in his burning of Atlanta, Lincoln wrote, "The undertaking being a great success, the honor is all yours."

William Gilmore Simms, an outstanding scholar of the Old South, was an eye-witness of Sherman's performance in helpless South Carolina. He recorded some details. The harshness of winter found scantily-clad people with only tents for shelter. Flames from burning villages hideously illuminated the night sky. For many of the populace the only available food was the garbage left where the Union troops had camped. Thousands, accustomed to plenty, were reduced to a ration of corn patiently gleaned from the ground where the invaders' horses had fed.

He gave some facts incident to the burning of Columbia. Scorning the consideration generally accorded womanhood, soldiers snatched articles of jewelry from their persons. Pleas to spare apparel of children fell on deaf ears as the garments went into the flames. In instances, even the sanctity of cemeteries was violated; graves were opened and caskets explored in search of treasure.

Lincoln had good reason to anticipate what would happen in South Carolina; it had just happened to Atlanta and Georgia!

In his second inaugural, the President intimated that Southern slaveholders were harsh masters. Then, **immediately preceding** the "with malice toward none" passage, he said:
"Yet, if God wills that the war continue until every drop of blood drawn by the lash **shall be paid by another drawn by the sword,** as was said three thousand years ago, so still it must be said 'the judgments of the Lord are true and righteous altogether.'"

After which, you are prepared to read again: "With malice toward none — with charity for all."

The Lincoln cult labors to build up a "friend of the South" theory, insisting that he desired to pay for the slaves. He did at one time indulge in talk of compensation — born in talk, it died in talk. It was Edgar Lee Masters, a Northern writer, who appraised Lincoln's real feeling toward the South as one of hidden and deep malignancy.

AN OLD SOLDIER SCORNS
TO EQUIVOCATE

IN 1861, after South Carolina's secession, a Union garrison held Fort Sumter at Charleston. Lincoln knew that the Confederates would resist its reinforcement. So, when he arranged to send an "expedition", he shrewdly camouflaged its mission as one to "provision" the garrison with food. Nevertheless, he actually ordered out to accompany it "steamers Pocahontas, Pawnee, and Harriet Lane", these to be supplied with guns and troops! It so happened that the Pocahontas and the Pawnee were warships, the Harriet Lane an armed cutter.

Lincoln overlooked, however, sharing his secret with the Commanding General of the Army. When, a few days later, General Scott carried out the order, he wrote Lieutenant-Colonel Scott:

"This letter will be handed you by Captain G. V. Fox, ex-officer of the Navy, and a gentleman of high standing, as well as possessed of extraordinary nautical ability. He is charged by high authority here with command of an expedition, under cover of certain ships of war, whose object is to reinforce Fort Sumter."

There spoke the soldier. With the bluntness of an old-timer, he came out flatly with the truth. He knew who was responsible for the movement — "high authority here." He gave the "steamers" their proper designation—"ships of war." He said nothing of "provisioning only", nor did he hedge as to the expedition's goal; he stated it with disarming directness, "to reinforce Fort Sumter."

UNCLE TOM'S CABIN

THIS SHREWDLY-CONCEIVED caricature of Southern slavery conditions fired a war-spirit in the North. It further contributed to the blocking of European recognition of the independence of the Confederate Government.

Albert J. Beveridge, Northerner and scholarly biographer of Lincoln, appraised the book. In his view, its apparent purpose was to convey the impression that its characters were representative Southern types; that, in general, the Southern man was overbearing and ruthless, the Southern woman a stranger to competence and Christian charity; that the slaves were frequently shamefully mistreated.

Hear another Northerner, Abraham Lincoln: "I have no prejudice against the Southern people. They are just what we would be in their situation. I surely will not blame them for not doing what I should not know how to do myself. If all earthly power were given me, I should not know what to do as to the existing institution of slavery."

Richard H. Wilmer was an Alabama Episcopal Bishop whose churches were padlocked by a Union officer. His **Reminiscences** contain some pungent observations. He noted that "the most striking character in the book, for honesty, fidelity, and piety", was Uncle Tom, a **product of the slavery system;** that its "most attractive character" was Eva, **a slaveholder;** that its "worst character" was Legree, "a **Northern man** who came South, trafficked in slaves, and maltreated them."

"HISTORY"!

CONSIDER A SAMPLE of "history" taught in Southern High Schools.

It relates that on the night of April 12, 1861 a group of secession enthusiasts headed by Roger Pryor visited Fort Sumter to demand immediate surrender of the garrison, a demand which its commander refused. Thereupon, dissatisfied with Major Anderson's attitude, with no notification to Confederate General Beauregard and without approval of Jefferson Davis, Pryor took it upon himself to order an attack, and the bombardment **began at once.** The paragraph ends with the information, "Neither Davis nor Lincoln had ordered it. It was war."

The OFFICIAL RECORD tells a different story. By instruction of Confederate Secretary of War Walker, Beauregard demanded evacuation of the Fort. Anderson declined to surrender but remarked on the hopelessness of his position. Thereupon, again by direction of Walker, Beauregard withdrew his demand, proposing that Anderson set his own date for leaving. The new proposal came to naught, whereupon **Beauregard's aides,** Chestnut and Lee, personally informed Anderson: "By the authority of Brigadier-General Beauregard, we have the honor to notify you that he will open the fire of his batteries on Fort Sumter within one hour from this time."

Note carefully the "history", that "Neither Davis nor Lincoln had ordered" the bombardment.

APPOMATTOX

THE ANSWER is tragically simple. The North had a white population four times as large as that of the South. The South had no army, no navy, no treasury, no adequate munitions plants, practically no manufacturing. In material resources the North was far superior. The Union Army overwhelmingly outnumbered the Confederates. Toward the end, General Grant reported: "The Rebels have now in their ranks their last man. They have robbed the cradle and the grave."

Another item has not had the notice it deserves. Toward the end of the struggle the Union soldiers held the deadly advantage of being armed with **Spencer repeating rifles.** Of this circumstance a distinguished Northern author, a student of war and warfare, has written: "Even the bravest, battlehardened Confederates could not stand up against a rifle which shot seven times, while theirs shot once. It was sheer murder."

There were other factors. Grant and Sherman and Sheridan had "converted into a barren waste" large areas of the South. In consequence, at the surrender General Lee remarked that his army was in a starving condition and asked Grant to provide his forces with subsistence.

Only men fighting for what they regarded a lofty principle would have endured the hardships of the Confederate soldier. There were times when the food supply ran so low as to reduce them to the extremity of eating horse and dog and rat. In instances, in winter campaigns, frozen roads so cruelly tortured bare feet that resort was had to carrying infantry in wagons. In other cases the men skinned dead mules to provide a substitute for shoes. At Petersburg, in 1865, various diseases crippled men whose starving bodies were easy prey. Overcoats gone, uniforms ragged, the men nearly froze while the opposing well-fed, warmly-clothed Union troops had their needs bountifully supplied.

"RECONSTRUCTION" –
A PROGRAM OF VENGEANCE

RECITAL OF the details of the full story can not be attempted here. Warning of what the conquerors had planned had come when a Massachusetts enthusiast urged that South Carolina, Georgia, and Florida "be set apart as the home of the Negro." Others of his stripe were willing to turn the South into a "graveyard of whites", a section governed by Negroes "upheld by Northern white bayonets."

Interested students should read "The Prostrate State", written by James S. Pike, born in Maine, a sincere abolitionist, former associate-editor of the New York Tribune, who visited South Carolina in 1873 for a first-hand study of the situation.

His discovery of unbelievable thievery and brazen corruption left him shocked, burning with indignation. He found in utter ruin a commonwealth with a distinguished record of culture and which had produced statesmen of of the highest caliber. He learned that the reign of terror of carpet-bagger and former-slave had proved so thorough that it was questionable whether there was anything "left to steal". Those in control he characterized as villains to be classed among the criminals of the world.

Had Mr. Pike broadened his investigation of the "reconstruction" orgy, the record in other seceding States was loaded with an abundance of like material.

SOME REASONS FOR SECESSION

From THE BEGINNING, North and South were uncongenial. The South was wholly agricultural, the North largely commercial. In religion, New England was Congregational, Virginia Anglican, Pennsylvania Quaker, Maryland Roman Catholic. Other antagonisms developed. New England offended with snobbish airs of superiority. Colonies imposed tariffs upon goods from other colonies. Later Congress enacted a "protective tariff" which enriched the North at the expense of other sections.

The North jealously resented the South's political dominance. In 1860 it led in the election of Lincoln who failed to receive a single electoral vote from the South. The victorious faction was openly hostile to Southern interests.

Next, certain "Abolitionists" took pains to incite Southern slaves to rise against their masters. They poured torrents of abuse on the slave-owners. They proclaimed that Southern planters were infamously immoral. They denounced the membership of a group of Southern churches as "incarnate fiends", "endorsers of crimes of depraved humanity." One enthusiast wrote that Southern young men came North to find wives because of fear that Southern girls were unworthy. Soon, slave-uprisings ushered in a nightmarish era.

Southerners became alarmed. They had voluntarily entered the Union; but now, with conditions becoming unbearable, they recalled Lincoln's pronouncement that "any people, anywhere" had the right "to shake off the existing government."

A Confederate soldier would likely have told you:

1. Our States entered the Union with the understanding that they had the right to withdraw when membership proved unhappy.

2. We were tired of being gypped by unfair tariff laws.

3. We were fed up with insane abuse from South-hating fanatics.

4. We had bought our slaves from the North,

only to learn later that it proposed to free them without a penny of compensation.

5. Northern fanatics had inspired murderous slave-uprisings. Why wait for more?

6. A rabidly-sectional party was in control at Washington.

7. We had no idea of making war. We planned to relieve the North from further association with us.

Lest you conclude that only Southerners believed that they had the right to go their own way and be let alone, bear in mind the view of Henry Cabot Lodge, a New England Brahmin. He said that as of the date of the adoption of the Constitution, it was universally regarded as an experiment, entered upon by the States, and from which any State "had the right peaceably to withdraw."

MEET JEFFERSON DAVIS

CERTAIN PEOPLE have carefully seen to it that you are well informed regarding Mr. Lincoln. And, it is quite likely that you've heard precious little about Mr. Davis. You may even be one of those who think that the less said of him, the better.

So, let's look briefly at Jefferson Davis.

Born in 1808, he was a cadet at West Point when he was sixteen years of age. He was there with Robert E. Lee.

During his early field service, "pneumonia left him with a facial neuralgia that sometimes blinded him. After 1831 he was never a man of robust health or of a normal nervous system."

Later, giving up his commission as Lieutenant, he returned to his plantation. "He soon developed a system that was almost a model in the relations of master and slaves. He gave the servant community a large measure of self-government, and left in its hands, through an interesting jury system, the trial of all petty offenders."

Soon after his election to Congress in 1845, we had war with Mexico. Back into the service he went as a Colonel of Infantry. "When General Zachary Taylor's reduced force was attacked at Buena Vista, a stand by the Mississippians saved the day for the American forces and made Davis something of a national figure."

Presently, his State sent him to the United States Senate. "Soon he was named Chairman of its Committee on Military Affairs."

More honors were to come. When Franklin Pierce of New Hampshire became President, he chose as his Secretary of War none other than Jefferson Davis, who "strengthened the coast defenses, enlarged the army, directed valuable surveys, introduced various betterments at West Point."

He re-entered the Senate in 1857 where the

country recognized him as "one of the foremost of Southern Democrats."

"Until after the election of Lincoln in November 1860, he never felt that circumstances justified a withdrawal from the Union."

"To his surprise and regret, he was unanimously chosen by the Confederate Congress to be Provisional President of the Confederate States of America."

For four years he was leader of the cause for which the South fought and it broke his heart when the soldiers in Gray were overwhelmed by vastly superior numbers and resources.

Taken captive at the end, they imprisoned him in Fortress Monroe. "During the early part of his imprisonment he was manacled and subjected to severities that impaired his health." Shackled like an animal, the tortures there endured by the delicate, enfeebled man were born of a venom rivalling the savagery of the Oriental.

In his declining years, he wrote **The Rise and Fall of the Confederate Government.** "an excellent review of the Constitutional questions underlying secession."

"He was imposing, near six feet in height, erect, thin, graceful in his movements. He had much dignity of manner and a fine voice, combined with unfailing personal courtesy."

"Well!", you are thinking, "this writer thinks highly of Mr. Davis." Perhaps you will agree, when you learn that of the statements in quotation marks above, every one is taken, not from some "Professional Southerner," but from as fair-minded a source as could be found, the **Encyclopaedia Britannica.**

Another detail may grip your interest. His captors indicted their prisoner for treason. He was helpless, his friends powerless to aid, the entire North blazing with anger. His foes had the prisoner, the indictment, the courts, the juries. They needed no evidence. A jury trial would have been another version of the lamb on trial before a pack of wolves.

Then, what happened?

They planned, and prepared for, the trial —
but it **never came!**

Why?

It began to dawn on his persecutors that a
pretty picture would result if there should issue
from the Nation's Highest Court the judgment
that no treason was involved, that there was
nothing criminal in his and his South's doing
what West Point had taught him in Rawle's
View of the Constitution, a text which declared
that **any State had the right to secede,** if it saw
fit to do so.

So, now you have met Jefferson Davis, gentleman, scholar, soldier, statesman, executive,
martyr. Really, you might find it worth while
to read more of him.

Jefferson Davis' Farewell Speech
to the U.S. Senate

"I have heard, with some surprise, for it seemed to me idle, the repetition of the assertion heretofore made that the cause of the separation was the election of Mr. Lincoln . . . but no individual had the power to produce the existing state of things. It was the purpose, the end; it was the declaration by himself and his friends, which constitute the necessity of providing new safeguards for ourselves. The man was nothing, save as he was the representative of opinions, of a policy, of purposes, of power, to inflict upon us those wrongs to which freemen never tamely submit.

"I have striven to avert the catastrophe which now impends over the country, unsuccessfully; and I regret it. For the few days which I may remain, I am willing to labor in order that that catastrophe shall be as little as possible destructive to public peace and prosperity. If you desire at this last moment to avert civil war, so be it. . . . If you will but allow us to separate from you peaceably, since we cannot live peaceably together . . . then there are many relations which may still subsist between us . . . which may be beneficial to you as well as to us.

"If you will not have it thus; if in the pride of power, if in contempt of reason and reliance upon force, you say we shall not go, but shall remain as subjects to you, then, gentlemen of the North, a war is to be inaugurated the like of which men have not seen. . . .

"Is there wisdom, is there patriotism in the land? If so, easy must be the solution of this question. If not, then Mississippi's gallant sons will stand like a wall of fire around their State; and I go hence, not in hostility to you, but in love and allegiance to her, to take my place among her sons. . . .

"Towards you individually, as well as to those whom you represent, I would that I had the power now to say there shall be peace between us forever. I would that I had the power now to say the intercourse and the commerce between the States, if they cannot live in one Union, shall still be uninterrupted; that all the social relations shall remain undisturbed; that the son in Mississippi shall visit freely his father in Maine, and the reverse; and that each shall be welcomed when he goes to the other, not by himself alone, but also by his neighbors; and that all that kindly intercourse which has subsisted between the different sections of the Union shall continue to exist. It is not only for the interest of all, but it is my profoundest wish, my sincerest desire, that such remnant of that which is passing away may grace the memory of a glorious, though too brief, existence. . . .

"Today it is in the power of two bad men, at the opposite ends of the telegraphic line between Washington and Charleston, to precipitate the State of South Carolina and the United States into a conflict of arms. . . .

"And still will you hesitate; still will you do nothing? Will you sit with sublime indifference and allow events to shape themselves? No longer can you say the responsibility is upon the Executive. He has thrown it upon you. He has notified you that he can do nothing. He has told you the responsibility now rests with Congress; and I close as I began, by invoking you to meet that responsibility, bravely to act the patriot's part. If you will, the angel of peace may spread her wings, though it be over divided States; and the sons of the sires of the Revolution may still go on in friendly intercourse with each other . . . and the happiness of all be still interwoven together. Thus may it be; and thus it is in your power to make it."

When Jefferson Davis had finished, the applause in the galleries was so tumultuous that the presiding officer shouted that the sergeant at arms would remove all disorderly persons. After quiet had been restored, a deep hush pervaded the Senate.

The silence was finally broken by Lincoln's friend Trumbull, the Republican Senator from Illinois. He rose to attack Davis' speech, for he feared the effect its moving eloquence might have on his cohorts. He was contemptuous of any appeal to let the seceding states go in peace, and scornful of the idea of withdrawing the small Federal garrison from Sumter to prevent an overt clash.

"Then, said Davis in the last reply he was ever to make to an opponent in the United States Senate, " I have to say to the Senator, his ideas of honor and my own are very different; that I should hold the man to be a scoundrel who did not desire to have a garrison withdrawn, if he believed that garrison might produce bloodshed and could not do good."

This is a portion of that 15,000 word speech.

Jefferson Davis' first address to the Confederate Congress.

"We protest solemnly in the face of mankind, that we desire peace at any sacrifice, save that of honor. In independence we seek no conquest, no aggrandizement, no concession of any kind from the States with which we have lately been confederated. All we ask is to be let alone--that those who never held power over us shall not now attempt our subjugation by arms. This we will, we must, resist to the direst extremity. The moment that this pretension is abandoned, the sword will drop from our grasp, and we shall be ready to enter into treaties of amnesty and commerce that cannot but be mutually beneficial. So long as this pretension is maintained, with a firm reliance on that Divine Power which covers with its protection the just cause, we must continue to struggle for our inherent right to freedom, independence, and self government."

"If the Declaration of Independence justified the secession of 3,000,000 Colonists in 1776 why did it not justify the secession of 5,000,000 Southerners from the Union in 1861.

Horace Greeley

How many states has the United States helped to secede from Russia and other nations since 1861?